THE GREAT™
AMERICAN
HISTORY
QUIZ

Americana

THE GREAT™
AMERICAN
HISTORY
QUIZ

Americana

Series Created by
Abbe Raven and Dana Calderwood

Written by
**Charles Norlander, Howard Blumenthal
and Dana Calderwood**

WARNER BOOKS

A Time Warner Company

Warner Books, Inc., 1271 Avenue of the Americas,
New York, NY 10020

Visit our Web site at www.twbookmark.com

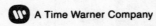 A Time Warner Company

Printed in the United States of America

Library of Congress Cataloging-in-Publication Data

   The great American history quiz. Americana / by the History Channel.
      p.   cm.
      ISBN: 0-7394-1429-1
      1. United States—History—Examinations, questions, etc.
   2. United States—History—Miscellanea.   I. History Channel
   (Television network)
   E178.25.G74   2000
   973'.076—dc21   00-031756

Cover design by Carolyn Lechter
Cover photograph by AP/Wide World Photos
Book design and text composition by Ralph Fowler

This edition of <u>The Great American History Quiz</u>™ is called "Americana." It will test your knowledge of general American history—from the most basic to the most arcane.

But before we jump into the history of our great country, here are a few questions about America before it became . . . well, America:

1 This Spanish explorer set off from Spain with 600 men in 1538 to search for gold in the New World. Though he didn't find gold, he did discover what is now known as the Mississippi River. The name of this intrepid Spaniard is:

(a) Francisco Vasquez de Coronado

(b) Francisco Pizarro

(c) Hernando Cortes

(d) Hernando de Soto

A N S W E R

(d) Hernando de Soto discovered the Mississippi in May 1541. Sadly, de Soto died a year after his discovery and was buried in the mud at the river's bottom.

2 Though he gave glory to Queen Elizabeth I by naming the settlement he helped finance after her, this English nobleman was executed in 1618 for treason. Who was it?

(a) Sir Walter Raleigh

(b) John White

(c) Sir Francis Drake

(d) John Smith

A N S W E R

(a) Though he named his settlement Virginia after the Virgin Queen, Sir Walter Raleigh was beheaded at Whitehall in 1618 for plotting to overthrow King James.

3 We all think we know the story of how the Pilgrims climbed aboard the *Mayflower* and made their way to the New World. But your question: Out of the 102 people on board, how many of them were actually Pilgrims?

(a) 0

(b) 50

(c) 80

(d) 102

ANSWER

(b) 50. The remaining 52 men, women, and children were still faithful to the Church of England.

4 Which one of the original thirteen colonies was settled primarily by people released from debtors' prisons?

(a) Maryland

(b) Connecticut

(c) Georgia

(d) North Carolina

4

A N S W E R

(c) James Ogelthorpe, an Oxford-educated humanitarian, established the colony of Georgia in 1732 to help "the industrious yet unfortunate poor."

5 One hundred years before Thomas Jefferson wrote the Declaration of Independence, another Virginian wrote his "Declaration of the People," which criticized the colonial government for levying unfair taxes and failing to protect the colonists from the threat of Indian attack. When the governor of Virginia failed to respond, this rabble-rouser got together a following and burned down Jamestown, forcing the governor to flee. Who was the instigator of one of the earliest revolts against British colonial rule?

(a) Nat Bacon

(b) Mary Dyer

(c) Jacob Leisler

(d) John Paxton

5

(a) Nat Bacon's 1676 rebellion against Governor Sir William Berkeley is considered the first substantial uprising against colonial governments.

Francis Scott Key wrote the music for "The Star-Spangled Banner." True or false?

6

ANSWER

Well, that's actually false, because he wrote the words in a wonderful poem, but he applied those words to an already existing melody. It was actually from an old British drinking song, "To Anacreon in Heaven."

7 And we all know that Francis Scott Key wrote the words to "The Star-Spangled Banner" while he watched a battle at Fort McHenry. But do you know what city Fort McHenry was built to protect?

(a) Baltimore, Maryland

(b) Arlington, Virginia

(c) Atlanta, Georgia

(d) Boston, Massachusetts

ANSWER

(a) Baltimore, Maryland. First used as a fort during the Revolutionary War, the fort remained in active military service until the last active garrison left on July 20, 1912.

8 Betsy Ross sewed the first official U.S. flag. True or false?

A N S W E R

False: There's no historical proof that Betsy Ross actually sewed the first U.S. flag. This popular legend seems to have been started by her grandson almost a century after Betsy allegedly threaded her way into history.

Speaking of the American flag, what is the only building in Washington, D.C., where the U.S. flag is flown around the clock?

(a) The White House

(b) The Capitol

(c) The Washington Monument

(d) The Vietnam Memorial

9

ANSWER

(b) The Capitol.

10 The name "Liberty Bell" was coined to honor the newly won liberty of our nation. Is that true or false?

10

ANSWER

False: The name "Liberty Bell" was coined
by the Anti-Slavery Movement in the 1830s,
and it referred to the liberty of blacks. In
fact, the whole popular legend of the Liberty
Bell was made up by a little-known author
in the 1840s. Until then, you see, no one had
even considered the bell to be a national
treasure.

11 Another little-known fact about the bell is that if you were able to ring it, it would chime in E-flat. If you wanted to risk imprisonment and find this out for yourself, where would you have to go to ring the bell?

(a) New York

(b) Philadelphia, Pennsylvania

(c) Boston, Massachusetts

A N S W E R

(b) Philadelphia, Pennsylvania. Interestingly enough, though, you'd really have to travel to *Pensylvania* to ring the bell—because the spelling of states' names wasn't standardized in 1752, the year the bell was cast. That's how the name of the state appears on the bell itself.

History is a collection of breathtaking stories, and we study it to understand who we are, what we do and why. History is more romantic and more exciting than any fiction. And it's part of a story . . . our story . . . that's not yet finished. Take, for example, stories of fame and fortune. Celebrities. And I'm not talking about Sinatra, or Streisand, or Elvis Presley. Superstardom is not a new idea, which is why our salute to American stardom begins 150 years ago.

12 One of the nineteenth century's brightest stars was the opera soprano Jenny Lind. Dubbed "the Swedish Nightingale," she was famous in Europe but almost unknown in the U.S. Then one person risked a fortune to promote a Jenny Lind tour in this country. The gamble paid off. Her first performance in 1850 drew thousands of people, and her nine months of concerts were a huge success. Who guided Jenny Lind to fame in the United States?

(a) Andrew Carnegie

(b) Gertrude Vanderbilt

(c) P. T. Barnum

Amazingly, he had never seen or heard Jenny Lind when he risked his entire fortune on her. But that didn't seem to matter to one of the greatest promoters of all times . . . P. T. Barnum.

13 Legend has it that Annie Oakley could shoot the head off a running quail when she was twelve years old. Whatever the truth of that tale, Oakley's sharpshooting skills made her an international star in Buffalo Bill's Wild West Show. There are many legendary stories about just how good a shot Annie was. In what may be the most famous story, she shot the ashes off a cigarette held in the lips of a national leader. Who was it?

(a) Kaiser Wilhelm II

(b) Teddy Roosevelt

(c) Czar Nicholas II

13

ANSWER

(a) Kaiser Wilhelm II. How did it happen? It seems he asked to participate with Oakley in the show while she was performing in Berlin.

His name was Rudolph Valentino, and his fame as the great lover in silent films made him a Hollywood legend. His handsome Latin looks inspired legions of wildly devoted fans. His big break came with the starring role in *The Four Horsemen of the Apocalypse*. How long did Valentino's career last?

(a) Three years

(b) Nine years

(c) Eighteen years

A N S W E R

(b) Nine years. His death triggered hysteria and even suicide among fans. There were riots at his funeral, and over 100,000 people lined up to view the coffin. And just for the record, Rudolph Valentino's full name was Rodolpho Alfonzo Rafaelo Pierre Filibert Guglielmi di Valentina d'Antonguolla. No kidding!

15 Erik Weisz may have been the most famous magician and escape artist who ever lived, but you probably know him better as Harry Houdini. A master of out-door spectacles and life-threatening magic, he took his stage name from Robert Houdin, a French magician he idolized as a boy. During World War I, Houdini put his talents to use for American troops. What did he do for them?

(a) Teach Marines how to catch bullets in their teeth

(b) Teach sailors how to survive for long periods under water

(c) Teach soldiers how to escape from handcuffs

15

(c) Houdini taught American soldiers how to escape from handcuffs. In later years, Houdini and his wife agreed to an experiment with the supernatural. The first to die would try to contact the survivor; but his wife, who outlived the great magician, said she never heard from Harry.

Remember this year: 1908. It plays mysteriously through this set of questions called "Dead, Alive, or Not Yet Born." We'll provide the name of a well-known American. Your job: to determine whether that person was dead, alive, or not yet born in 1908. You understand the concept? Good. Okay.

16 Were famed outlaws Bonnie and Clyde dead, alive, or not yet born in 1908?

16

ANSWER

Bonnie and Clyde were gunned down by police in 1934. But they were not yet born in the year ... you guessed it: 1908.

Was Alexander Graham Bell, the inventor of the telephone, dead, alive, or not yet born in the year 1908?

The answer is that Alexander Graham Bell was alive in 1908. He didn't die until 1922, or so we understand. Because it was a phone call that came through and delivered the death notice.

18 The founder of the Otis Elevator Company was Elijah Graves Otis. Was Otis in his grave in 1908?

18

ANSWER

Elijah Otis was already dead in 1908. Sad to say, he passed away in 1861.

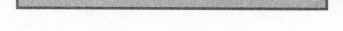

Was women's rights leader Elizabeth Cady Stanton dead, alive, or not yet born in 1908?

19

Elizabeth Cady Stanton led the fight for women's suffrage, but didn't live to see it happen. She was already dead in 1908.

How about famed jazz singer Billie Holiday? Was she dead, alive, or not yet born in 1908?

20

Billie Holiday's birth year was 1915, so she was not yet born in 1908.

★ ★ ★ ★ ★ ★ ★ ★

21 And finally, he's the only U.S. president to serve two nonconsecutive terms in office. Was Grover Cleveland dead, alive, or not yet born in 1908?

21

ANSWER

If you said "not yet born" you are incorrect. However, if you said either "alive" or "dead," you're absolutely right. That's because Grover Cleveland was each of those for one half of 1908. He died on June 24 of that year.

Through the first half of the 1770s, King George III was having an impossible time with Parliament. A group of rabble-rousers was also making his life miserable by talking about revolution in the American colonies. Today we call these men our Founding Fathers. "Listen my children, and you shall hear, of the midnight ride of Paul Revere." And what a famous ride it was. Revere, along with some others we now call Patriots, was responsible for warning the provincial Congress about the approach of British troops. Your question:

 22 Who was the general who led those British forces?

(a) William Howe

(b) Charles Cornwallis

(c) Thomas Gage

22

Paul Revere's ride was sparked by the approach of troops commanded by answer **(c)** General Thomas Gage. Gage ordered the march of the Redcoats on Lexington and Concord in search of munitions, as well as, some historians think, Samuel Adams, the leading revolutionary agitator. The British forces met the minutemen, and the American Revolution began.

★ ★ ★ ★ ★ ★ ★ ★

23 But before General Gage sparked Paul Revere's famous ride, he had a pretty good day job as the governor of one of the colonies. Which colony was General Gage the governor of?

(a) Massachusetts

(b) New Hampshire

(c) New Jersey

(d) Delaware

23

(a) Before the Revolutionary War, Thomas Gage was sitting pretty as the governor of Massachusetts.

24 We've all heard about "The shot heard 'round the world" that got the Revolutionary War going. When the British Army tried to get past a group of minutemen, an unordered shot rang out, causing a bit of a ruckus, and by the end of the melee, eight minutemen had lost their lives. Many consider this to be the beginning of the Revolutionary War. Where was "the shot heard 'round the world" fired?

(a) Concord, Massachusetts

(b) Lexington, Massachusetts

(c) Saratoga, New York

(d) Trenton, New Jersey

24

(b) The shot heard 'round the world was fired in Lexington, Massachusetts. To this day, no one knows whether the British or the Patriots fired that first shot.

25 Perhaps no founding father matched Ben Franklin's range of contributions to our American way of life. Many community organizations that we now take for granted were originally promoted by Franklin. Which of the following institutions is the only one not associated with Ben Franklin?

(a) Fire company

(b) Hospital

(c) ASPCA

(d) Public library

(e) Post office

25

Well, it seems that there wasn't much that Ben Franklin didn't do. This colorful founding father was a statesman, diplomat, writer, editor, scientist, and inventor. In fact, the only institution we just mentioned that is not associated with Ben Franklin is answer **(c)** ASPCA.

26 Artist Emanuel Leutze created the familiar depiction of George Washington crossing the Delaware River. The question is, which way was George going?

(a) From Pennsylvania to New Jersey

(b) From New Jersey to Pennsylvania

(c) From Delaware to Pennsylvania

26

ANSWER

On Christmas night 1776, Washington snuck across the Delaware River from Pennsylvania, for a stunning surprise attack that became known as the Battle of Trenton. Washington's victory was a huge morale booster. So the answer is **(a)**: He crossed from Pennsylvania to New Jersey. And by the way, if you answered (c), you lose history points *and* geography points: You can't get from Delaware to Pennsylvania by crossing a river.

27 "Don't fire till you see the whites of their eyes!" is easily one of the most quotable lines of the American Revolution. It was an order given by one of the wittier (and more economic) patriot commanders in order to save ammunition during the Battle of Bunker Hill. So here's a question about that famous battle. True or false: The Battle of Bunker Hill actually took place on Bunker Hill.

27

A N S W E R

Surprisingly, the answer is false: Most of the fighting at the Battle of Bunker Hill actually took place on nearby Breed's Hill.

28 In 1781 the British surrendered at Yorktown, Virginia. But the ceremony leading up to the historic event was anything but simple. To whom did the British officially surrender?

(a) Washington

(b) Lincoln

(c) Eisenhower

(d) none of the above

28

(b) Lincoln . . . General Benjamin Lincoln. Here's what happened: The British General Cornwallis feigned illness to avoid surrendering and sent General O'Hara in his place. At first O'Hara tried surrendering to General Rochambeau, the French commander. But Rochambeau directed him to Washington. Then Washington sent the British general to Lincoln, who had been humiliated by the British when he was forced to give up the city of Charlestown. So it was Benjamin Lincoln who accepted the British surrender at Yorktown.

29 One can only imagine the scramble that took place after the Declaration of Independence was drafted: a bunch of old men fighting each other to be the first to sign it. Who clawed his way to the front of the room to be the first person to endorse this all important document?

(a) Benjamin Franklin

(b) Samuel Adams

(c) Thomas Jefferson

(d) John Hancock

29

(d) The first, and most visible, signature on the Declaration of Independence is that of John Hancock.

Many of our founding fathers had a way with words. In the next two questions, see if you can match up the famous phrase with the American Patriot who said it.

 30 Which of our founding fathers reportedly said: "I only regret that I have but one life to give for my country"?

(a) Nathan Hale

(b) Benedict Arnold

(c) Ethan Allan

(d) George Washington

30

(a) Nathan Hale. Although no one thought to officially document this famous phrase, rumor has it that Nathan Hale uttered these words just before he was hanged by the British for espionage.

31 Which of our founding fathers is reported to have said "I have not yet begun to fight" while battling the British warship *Serapis*?

(a) John Paul Jones

(b) Henry Knox

(c) Patrick Henry

(d) Thomas Paine

31

(a) Those words belong to one of America's early naval heroes: Scottish-born patriot John Paul Jones.

**George Washington once said: "It is not my cus-
tom to keep money to look at." A large number
of Americans think that way today. Perhaps
there's even one in your family. We are going
to time-travel to several eras in history and
learn about the cost of living. Prepare to be
depressed!**

 Prices have changed a lot over the
years. Let's see how well you do as a
historical shopper. We'll begin in 1896
with three items that were being advertised in the
newspapers that year: a Columbia bicycle, an
Anderson typewriter, and a Singer sewing machine
with a complete set of attachments. Your question:

Which item was priced at $9?

Which was $25?

And which one would have cost you $100?

32

Back in 1896, our big-ticket item was the Columbia bicycle. It sold for $100. The Anderson typewriter would have cost you $25. That means that the Singer sewing machine, with attachments, was advertised for $9 in 1896.

33 Now let's jump ahead to the year 1923. This time you're buying a lawnmower advertised in the *New York Times*, a Kodak camera, and a steamship ticket from New York to Boston. Your question:

Which item is priced at about $5?

Which one at about $10?

And which item is priced at $50?

33

In 1923, the New England mower from James McCreary & Company sold for about $10. The Kodak #1 camera was priced at $50. And the steamship ticket would have cost you $5.19. The year 1923 was also an exciting one for debuts: The Butterfinger candy bar was introduced, and the Popsicle was patented.

★ ★ ★ ★ ★ ★ ★ ★

Just after World War II, America was busy getting back to work, and making more babies than ever before. We're talking about the 1950s, when America discovered the potent combination of sex, drugs, and rock and roll.

34 In the decade of Marilyn Monroe, *Playboy*, and *Lolita*, no fantasy was as shocking as the honest truth. According to the Kinsey Report of 1948 and 1953, over 80 percent of American males had engaged in premarital sex. What was the percentage for females?

(a) 20 percent

(b) 35 percent

(c) 50 percent

34

(c) According to noted sex researcher Alfred Kinsey, 50 percent of females had engaged in premarital sex during the "innocent" decade of the 1950s.

35 In 1951, the father of eight-year-old Linda Brown began a lawsuit against the Topeka, Kansas, Board of Education which eventually found its way up to the Supreme Court. What did the Court decide in the landmark case of *Brown* v. *The Board of Education*?

(a) That racial segregation in public schools was illegal

(b) That evolution could be taught in public schools

(c) That prayer was not allowed in public schools

(d) That separate but equal schools for black and white children was fair

35

(a) In *Brown* v. *The Board of Education*, the Supreme Court ruled that racial segregation in public schools was illegal. Not bad for an eight-year-old girl.

36 A reflection of the times, one of the popular products of the 1950s was what *Time* magazine called "Don't Give a Damn Pills." The tranquilizer Meprobamate was a new kind with manageable side effects. They were prescribed to ease tension and anxiety, and by 1959, tranquilizer sales had soared to $5 million annually, with suburban women first in line. What was the commercial brand name of the popular Meprobamate tranquilizer?

(a) Equinox

(b) Miltown

(c) Thorazine

A N S W E R

(b) Miltown.

37 According to noted music historian Charlie Gillette, the first rock-and-roll singer to make *Billboard*'s National Best-Sellers Chart was crazy, man, crazy. Who was the performer?

(a) Bill Haley and the Comets

(b) Ray Charles

(c) Willie Dixon

(d) Big Joe Turner

37

ANSWER

(a) Bill Haley and the Comets. The record was released in 1953, the hit was followed by "Shake Rattle and Roll" in 1954, and then "Rock Around the Clock" in 1955. Of course, black musicians were making rock-and-roll records as early as the 1940s.

38 This 1950s story actually started in the late 1940s. On Long Island, New York, the American Dream was being built one neighborhood at a time. In 1947, the company of Levitt & Sons, housebuilders, had a great idea: They started building assembly-line housing and developed a planned community called Levittown. Levittown offered suburban living for average Americans. With low-cost homes, it became a symbol of the suburbs following World War II. How much living space was in the original Levittown home?

(a) About 700 square feet

(b) About 1,100 square feet

(c) About 1,500 square feet

38

ANSWER

(a) An original Levittown home was 720 square feet. That included two bedrooms, a kitchen, a living room, a bathroom, and closets, and it sold for—get this—just under $7,000.

The next category is "Disasters."

 Imagine facing a raging wall of water 40 feet high, moving 40 miles an hour—a wall of water so powerful it tosses a 48-ton locomotive a mile. Well, that's just what the people of Johnstown, Pennsylvania, faced during the Great Johnstown Flood. Thousands of people perished in the disaster, which was triggered when a dam collapsed after heavy rains. Name the decade in which it happened.

(a) The 1850s

(b) The 1880s

(c) The 1910s

39

The Johnstown Flood occurred in 1889, so the correct answer is **(b)** the 1880s. The dam had been built to provide a good place to fish; but when it collapsed, 2,000 people lost their lives.

In what year did approximately 7,000 people lose their lives during the hurricane that struck Galveston Island, Texas, the deadliest national disaster in U.S. history?

(a) 1853

(b) 1900

(c) 1912

(d) 1922

ANSWER

(b) The Great Galveston Island Hurricane struck in 1900.

41 What volcano erupted on May 18, 1980, killing fifty-seven people?

(a) Kilauea Volcano, Hawaii

(b) Mount St. Helens, Washington

(c) Augustine Volcano, Arkansas

(d) Mount Wrangell, Alaska

ANSWER

(b) Mount St. Helens, Washington.

42 Mobs of Union soldiers, just freed from Confederate prisons, piled aboard the steamboat *Sultana* to head north on the Mississippi River. The boat was dangerously overcrowded, setting the scene for the worst maritime disaster in U.S. history. It happened when a boiler exploded, turning the steamboat into a fiery wreck. Now the question: How many lives were lost on the *Sultana*?

(a) About 400

(b) About 1,000

(c) About 1,500

42

(c) The official death toll was 1,547 lives. That's more lives than were lost on the *Titanic*. Oh, by the way, how overcrowded was the *Sultana*? Its safe capacity was 376 passengers.

43 During the 1830s, U.S. troops forced Native Americans from their Georgia land so local whites could have it. Then the tribe was forced to march from Georgia to what is now Oklahoma. Thousands died from sickness, hunger, and exposure along the way. This brutal six-month journey became known as the Trail of Tears. Which Native American people endured this tragedy?

(a) The Cherokee

(b) The Algonquin

(c) The Comanche

43

(a) The Cherokee. The Supreme Court had ruled that the Cherokee land in Georgia legally belonged to the Cherokee people, but, amazingly, President Jackson refused to enforce the ruling, setting the stage for the Trail of Tears.

44 On April 19, 1995, a truck bomb exploded outside a federal building in Oklahoma City. The death toll made it the single worst terrorist incident in U.S. history. The exact date of the blast marked the second anniversary of another tragic event. What was it?

(a) World Trade Center bombing

(b) Federal raid at Waco

(c) Federal raid at Ruby Ridge

44

(b) The federal raid at Waco, Texas. Many investigators felt that the date was no coincidence. They believed the Oklahoma City bombing was a right-wing reprisal for the federal actions at Waco.

America has had two presidents named Johnson. We're going to ask you a question, and you determine whether the answer is our thirty-sixth president—Lyndon Baines Johnson—or our seventeenth president, Andrew Johnson. We call this category "Johnson & Johnson." Okay, here we go.

 As president, he signed a bill authorizing the use of the metric system in the U. S.

Was that Andrew Johnson or Lyndon Johnson?

45

Hard to believe, but Andrew Johnson signed that bill into law back in 1866. And now, 133 years later, you can actually buy soda in liter-size bottles. Who says Congress can't get things done?

46 He was born into a very poor family and worked as a schoolteacher for a while.

Is this Lyndon Johnson or Andrew Johnson?

46

The answer: Lyndon Johnson. He was the eldest of five children and was raised in a modest cabin, and he was also a high school teacher in Houston, Texas.

47 He was the first president to be impeached.

Am I talking about Lyndon Johnson or Andrew Johnson?

47

A N S W E R

Andrew Johnson.

48 Both Johnsons became president following an assassination. Who spoke these words after taking office? "The greatest leader of our time has been struck down by the foulest deed of our time."

Was that Andrew Johnson or
Lyndon Johnson?

48

The answer is Lyndon Johnson, and his address before a joint session of Congress continued. Today, John Fitzgerald Kennedy lives on in the immortal words and works he left behind.

49 If you were on society's A-list in 1886, you might have received an invitation to the opening ceremonies for the new Statue of Liberty. French sculptor Frédéric-Auguste Bartholdi faced enormous challenges in creating the Statue of Liberty. Her copper skin was thinner than the thickness of two pennies. It would uphold the statue's immense size and weight, so an internal structure was critical for support. And what's more, the entire statue would be shipped across the Atlantic. To solve these formidable problems, Bartholdi hired a master builder who constructed an interior framework that could be reassembled after the voyage. Who was this master builder?

(a) Ferris wheel builder George Ferris

(b) Eiffel Tower builder Alexander-Gustave Eiffel

(c) Brooklyn Bridge builder John Roebling

49

ANSWER

(b) Alexander-Gustave Eiffel.

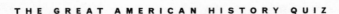

50 Bartholdi promised to have the statue ready in time for America's Centennial celebration in 1876. Unfortunately, things didn't work out quite as planned. Bartholdi almost missed the 1876 deadline but managed to ship a part of the statue to Philadelphia for the exhibition. Which part of Lady Liberty's body made it to the United States on time?

(a) Her head

(b) Her torch

(c) Her book

(d) Her pedestal

50

(b) Her torch. Mounted on her pedestal, the Statue of Liberty was finally dedicated on October 28, 1886. But in a way, she still wasn't complete....

51 Emma Lazarus wrote her famous poem "The New Colossus" in 1883. But it wasn't affixed to the Statue of Liberty until 1903. Complete the famous line from her poem: "Give me your tired, your poor, your huddled masses yearning to breathe free.... I lift my lamp ..."

(a) "Above your glorious harbor"

(b) "And glow with the light of liberty"

(c) "Beside the golden door"

(d) "With pride and not prejudice"

51

ANSWER

The correct answer is **(c)**. Emma Lazarus wrote: "I lift my lamp beside the golden door." Lazarus was inspired to write this poem as she observed immigrants struggling to make a life in America. She believed that America was a place where everyone deserved a chance. In time, the statue became a symbol of the ideal of freedom and opportunity for all, an ideal that attracts people to our shores down to this very day.

52 No question about it—Lady Liberty is one hefty gal. She's 111'1" from the tip of her toes to the top of her head, and weighs a far-from-ladylike 156 tons. Her waist size is nothing to sneeze at either—how thick is her waist?

(a) 15 feet thick

(b) 35 feet thick

(c) 50 feet thick

(d) 75 feet thick

52

(b) 35 feet thick. That's about a size 220 in jeans.

We'll list some famous events in history that all happened in the same year. Your job is to name the year in which these events occurred.

53 This was a year when things were on the rise. American involvement in Vietnam escalated when a Navy ship allegedly was bombed in the Gulf of Tonkin. The Beatles' popularity skyrocketed as they arrived in New York City to begin their first U.S. tour. And Sidney Poitier's star reached new heights when he was the first black actor handed an Academy Award for Best Actor.

In what year did this happen?

53

A N S W E R

All of these events occurred in the year 1964.

54 Upton Sinclair published *The Jungle*, an exposé of the meat-packing industry. San Francisco suffered one of the worst earthquakes in U.S. history, which caused $400 million worth of property damages. Kellogg's sold Corn Flakes for the first time.

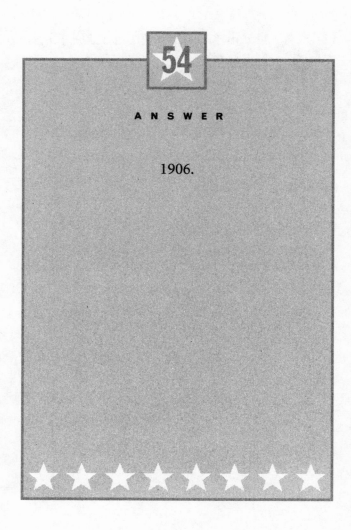

54

A N S W E R

1906.

55 Massachusetts became the first state to adopt a minimum wage. The Bull Moose Party was formed to reelect Theodore Roosevelt as president. The *Titanic*, the largest passenger ship in the world at the time, sank on its maiden voyage.

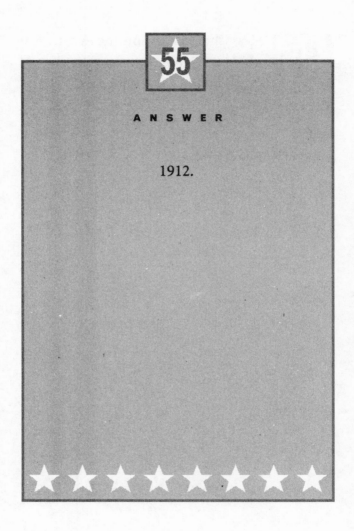

55

A N S W E R

1912.

56 The first pop-up toaster went on sale. Charles Lindbergh became the first man to fly solo across the Atlantic Ocean. American hero Babe Ruth hit 60 home runs, breaking the season record. Gertrude Ederle became the first woman to swim across the English Channel.

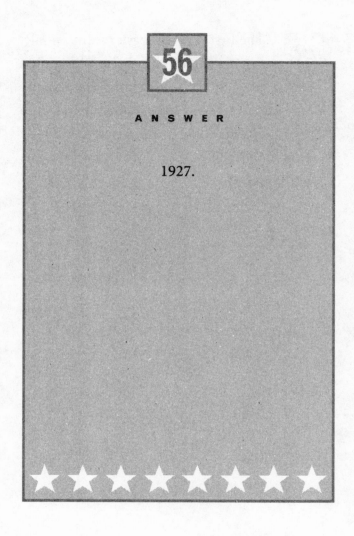

56

ANSWER

1927.

57 IBM launched the first personal computer. The AIDS virus was identified by scientists. The 52 Americans who had been held hostage in Iran for 444 days were released. President Reagan was shot in the chest as he was getting into his limousine.

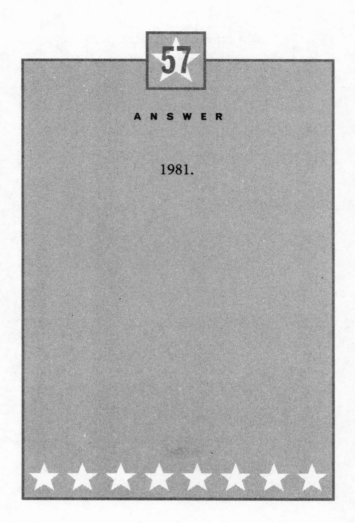

57

A N S W E R

1981.

58 During this year, in the 1930s, the sky was the limit. Howard Hughes flew around the globe in almost half the time it had taken anybody before. Orson Welles's radio program *War of the Worlds* convinced America that it was being invaded by aliens. And the Man of Steel made his debut in comic books around the country.

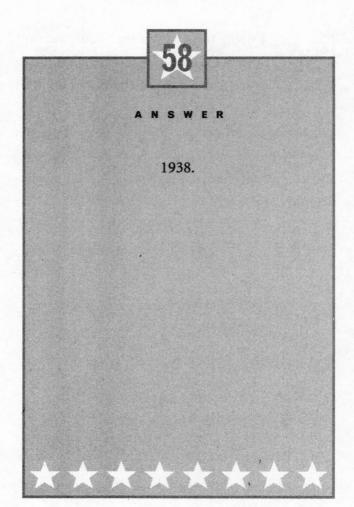

58

A N S W E R

1938.

"Four score and seven years ago" . . . **"Ask not what your country can do for you"** . . . **"I have a dream"** . . . **"Where's the beef?"** The next several questions are about words, written or spoken by a diverse group of Americans. Most are famous. One is a president. Another is a historical footnote, but you'll recognize what he said. We'll supply the quotation, your mission is to identify who said it.

59 Here's a quote that's sure to liven up your next family reunion: "Mothers are a biological necessity. Fathers are a social invention." Who said it?

(a) Mae West

(b) Susan B. Anthony

(c) Margaret Mead

59

(c) This quote is from cultural anthropologist Margaret Mead, famed for her outspokenness.

★ ★ ★ ★ ★ ★ ★ ★

60 "Yesterday, December 7, 1941—a date which will live in infamy—the United States of America was suddenly and deliberately attacked by Naval and Air Forces of the Empire of Japan."

(a) Franklin Delano Roosevelt

(b) General MacArthur

(c) Harry Truman

(d) George S. Patton

60

ANSWER

(a) Franklin Delano Roosevelt.

61 "To be great is to be misunderstood."

(a) Walt Whitman

(b) Henry David Thoreau

(c) Denis Leary

(d) Ralph Waldo Emerson

61

ANSWER

(d) Ralph Waldo Emerson.

62 "Mankind must put an end to war, or war will put an end to mankind."

(a) John F. Kennedy

(b) Harry Truman

(c) Woodrow Wilson

(d) Dwight D. Eisenhower

62

A N S W E R

(a) John F. Kennedy.

63 "Government of the people, by the people, for the people, shall not perish from the Earth."

(a) George Washington

(b) Thomas Jefferson

(c) Abraham Lincoln

(d) Franklin Delano Roosevelt

63

ANSWER

(c) Abraham Lincoln.

64 "If we don't succeed, we run the risk of failure."

(a) Ronald Reagan

(b) Dwight D. Eisenhower

(c) Dan Quayle

(d) Bill Clinton

64

A N S W E R

(c) Dan Quayle.

65 Our next quote offers this comment about television: "A medium, so called because it is neither rare nor well done." Who said that?

(a) Ernie Kovacs

(b) Marshall McLuhan

(c) Jack Paar

65

(a) Before there was Monty Python, before there was *Laugh-In*, there was the witty Ernie Kovacs.

66 Here's a wartime quote you probably heard: "Praise the Lord and pass the ammunition." Chaplain Howell Forgy was the person who said it. Name the war in which he was quoted.

(a) U.S. Civil War

(b) Spanish-American War

(c) World War I

(d) World War II

66

When a Japanese plane was hit during the attack on Pearl Harbor, Chaplain Forgy called out, "Praise the Lord and pass the ammunition." So the correct answer is **(d)**. He said it during World War II.

67 Continuing with wartime quotes, who said the following: "There is nothing more foolish than to think war can be stopped by war. You don't prevent anything by war except peace"?

(a) Dwight D. Eisenhower

(b) General George Patton

(c) Harry Truman

67

(c) Harry Truman. In his memoirs, the former president expressed his opinions about the notion of a so-called preventive war.

68

And now our final quote: "Injustice anywhere is a threat to justice everywhere." Who said it?

(a) Dr. Martin Luther King, Jr.

(b) Franklin D. Roosevelt

(c) Walter Cronkite

68

He spent his life fighting injustice, and when he received the Nobel Peace Prize in 1964, he was the youngest man ever to receive that honor. The correct answer is **(a)** Dr. Martin Luther King, Jr.

69 Social change is often sparked by troublemakers. And often these controversial agitators become heroes of future generations. Music can be a powerful agent for social change. Woody Guthrie understood music's power completely. His folk music often criticized political injustice and poverty. A phrase was written on the face of Woody's guitar because he believed a musical instrument could be a potent weapon. What was that phrase?

(a) "A weapon on the side of freedom"

(b) "This machine kills fascists"

(c) "This machine surrounds hate and forces it to surrender"

69

(b) "This machine kills fascists." If you answered (c), "This machine surrounds hate and forces it to surrender," you were close, because that's the sentence written on Pete Seeger's banjo.

70 In 1965, one book changed the U.S. auto industry forever. That book was *Unsafe at Any Speed*, written by Ralph Nader. In the book, Nader severely criticized automakers for building unsafe cars. He singled out one model in particular as a death trap. Now which car was it?

(a) The Corvair

(b) The Corvette

(c) The Pinto

70

A N S W E R

(a) The Corvair became infamous for unsafe design after Nader's book was published. One year later, his writings led to the passage of the National Traffic and Motor Vehicle Safety Act, which gave the government the power to set auto safety standards.

71 The pen truly is mightier than the sword: His widely read pamphlet *Common Sense* was responsible for convincing many American colonists to push for independence. Who are we talking about here?

(a) Thomas Paine

(b) Benjamin Franklin

(c) Alexander Hamilton

(d) Thomas Jefferson

71

ANSWER

(a) Thomas Paine was the author of the incredibly influential pamphlet, which was originally published anonymously and went on to sell over half a million copies—it was one of America's first best-sellers.

72 He led an unsuccessful slave rebellion in 1831, killing sixty whites and striking fear into the hearts of slave owners throughout the South. Who was he?

(a) William Lloyd Garrison

(b) Nat Turner

(c) Dred Scott

(d) Gabriel Prosser

72

(b) Nat Turner was the extremely influential slave who took on mythic proportions after his 1831 slave rebellion failed and he was hanged.

73 When Lincoln met this woman in 1862, he purportedly said "So you're the little woman that wrote the book that made this great war." Her novel *Uncle Tom's Cabin*, which sold over 300,000 copies the first year it was published in its entire form, shook the conscience of the world with its depiction of what life as a slave was really like. What is her name?

(a) Harriet Tubman

(b) Harriet Beecher Stowe

(c) Harriet Mitchell

(d) Elizabeth Cady Stanton

73

(b) The woman who wrote this famous book was Harriet Beecher Stowe.

★ ★ ★ ★ ★ ★ ★ ★

74 Almost 100 years later, another opinionated woman galvanized American consciousness with her book *The Feminine Mystique*, which urged women to question their second-class status in American society. Who was this rabble-rousing woman?

(a) Betty Friedan

(b) Gloria Steinem

(c) Germaine Greer

(d) Lucretia Mott

ANSWER

(a) Betty Friedan was the author of this seminal feminist book. She eventually went on to become one of the founders of NOW and helped set off a decade of protests, bra-burning, and the struggle for the Equal Rights Amendment. Not bad for a one-time suburban housewife.

This next category is a bit of a grab bag ... just a series of random questions and answers you'll find interesting.

 Jackie Robinson was the first black player in the Major Leagues: true or false?

75

False: Moses Fleetwood Walker was the first black player in the Majors, back in 1884. But then a silent agreement among club owners kept baseball segregated for decades. Jackie Robinson brought a public end to that segregation.

76 Attempting to clear his name after being accused of mismanaging $18,000 during his time as a senator, Richard Nixon went on national television and delivered one of his most famous speeches, one which included a reference to his little cocker spaniel. What was the name of this soon-to-be presidential pooch?

(a) Rover

(b) Checkers

(c) Socks

(d) Spot

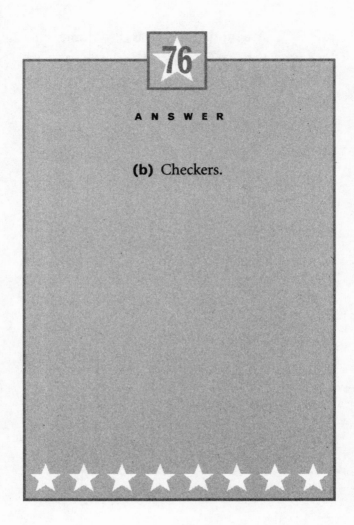

76

ANSWER

(b) Checkers.

77 Which New England state constitution is the oldest written constitution still in effect?

(a) Vermont

(b) Massachusetts

(c) Rhode Island

ANSWER

(b) Massachusetts.

78 What is the oldest city in America?

(a) St. Augustine, Florida

(b) Jamestown, Virginia

(c) Plymouth, Massachusetts

(d) Williamsburg, Virginia

78

ANSWER

(a) St. Augustine was established in 1565 by Don Pedro Menendez de Aviles, making it the oldest permanent European settlement on the North American continent.

79 The oldest state capitol still in continuous use is the one in

(a) Annapolis, Maryland

(b) Albany, New York

(c) Dover, Delaware

(d) Boston, Massachusetts

79

(a) The Maryland Statehouse, built in 1772, is the oldest U.S. capitol still in legislative use, and was the U.S. capitol briefly in 1783. Annapolis is also the home of the U.S. Naval Academy, St. John's College, and some amazing seafood restaurants.

80 Rice-A-Roni may have made San Francisco's trolleys famous, but streetcar aficionados know that the oldest continuously operating streetcars in the country are found in this Deep South city:

(a) Atlanta, Georgia

(b) Charleston, South Carolina

(c) Richmond, Virginia

(d) New Orleans, Louisiana

80

(d) New Orleans, Louisiana, has the oldest continuously operating streetcars in the country. They're a great, safe way to get around after you spend too much time drinking on Bourbon Street during Mardi Gras.

In a country of 275 million people, it's nice to know that some of our states can get some peace and quiet. Which lonely state is the only one that borders only one other state?

(a) New Hampshire

(b) Maine

(c) Hawaii

(d) Alaska

ANSWER

(b) Maine. (Being true loners, Alaska and Hawaii don't border any other states!)

82 And while we're on the subject of states, most people are aware that Alaska and Hawaii were the last two states admitted to the Union. But which state was #48?

(a) Oklahoma

(b) New Mexico

(c) Arizona

(d) Oregon

82

ANSWER

(c) Arizona was the forty-eighth state admitted to the Union. It joined the other forty-seven states on February 14, 1912.

83 And though California is farther west than Arizona, it was actually admitted to the Union years earlier, in 1850. Your question is this: What was California named after?

(a) A tree

(b) A Spanish novel

(d) Christopher Columbus's wife

(d) An Indian expression

83

ANSWER

(b) In 1506 Count Ordones de Montalvo published a book titled *Las Sergas de Esplandian,* a romantic novel that featured a warrior queen named Califia, who came from a mythical island named California.

84 What state capitol has a Confederate monument on its grounds?

(a) Nashville, Tennessee

(b) Charleston, West Virginia

(c) Montgomery, Alabama

(d) Columbia, South Carolina

84

(c) The capitol in Montgomery, Alabama, was the first capitol of the Confederacy. It still has a Confederate monument on its grounds.

85 You'd think that with what they charge for tuition, the Ivy League university that administers the Pulitzer Prize would award more than a $5,000 prize. What university gives out these coveted awards?

(a) Harvard University

(b) Columbia University

(c) Princeton University

(d) Yale University

85

A N S W E R

(b) Columbia University has been distributing the awards since 1917.

86 Where is the oldest medical school in the United States?

(a) University of Pennsylvania

(b) Harvard University

(c) William and Mary

(d) Yale

86

A N S W E R

(a) University of Pennsylvania is home of the oldest medical school in the United States. Fortunately, the medical school has updated all of its equipment since it was founded in 1740.

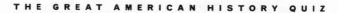

87 Americans are always on the lookout for a bargain. Manhattan was purchased from the Indians for $24 and a handful of beads; Andrew Johnson bought Alaska from Russia at the bargain-basement price of 2 cents an acre. We got an equally good deal on the Louisiana Purchase—the president at the time virtually doubled the size of the country at the price of 4 cents an acre. Who was this savvy shopper?

(a) Thomas Jefferson

(b) James Madison

(c) James Monroe

(d) John Adams

87

ANSWER

(a) Thomas Jefferson made the Louisiana Purchase in 1803.

88 For almost 50 years, Al Jolson entertained audiences as a singer, actor, and blackface comedian. He started in vaudeville, moved on to musicals, and then capped his career with films. Jolson is best remembered for his starring role in *The Jazz Singer*. It was the first feature talkie, and it revolutionized the movie business back in 1927. In his final performance, Jolson entertained American troops. Which war were they fighting at the time?

(a) World War II

(b) The Korean War

(c) The Vietnam War

88

Al Jolson performed up to the year of his death in 1950, so the correct answer is **(b)**. He last performed entertaining troops during the Korean War.

89 It's a policy named after a president. It's often called a cornerstone of the U.S. foreign policy. It announced that the Americas were no longer open to colonization by European powers. Which policy is this?

89

A N S W E R

The Monroe Doctrine. The policy was first outlined by President James Monroe in 1823 during a speech to Congress, but it wasn't called the Monroe Doctrine until 1853.

The U.S. declared independence on July 4, 1776. True or false?

90

False: The U.S. did not declare independence on July 4, 1776. Here's what really happened: The Continental Congress officially declared independence on July 2, but Jefferson's Declaration of Independence was dated and adopted on July 4. So we've come to celebrate the document rather than the actual event.

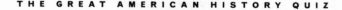

91 Who was the first U.S. president born in a hospital?

(a) Jimmy Carter

(b) John F. Kennedy

(c) Bill Clinton

ANSWER

(a) Jimmy Carter. In the early twentieth century, it was uncommon for anyone to be born in a hospital . . . even infants born to wealthy families like the Kennedys. Most people were born at home. Jimmy Carter's mother was a nurse, which may be why he was born in a hospital.

92 In 1870, Hiram Rebels became the first black U.S. senator. Whose vacant seat was he elected to fill?

(a) Ulysses S. Grant

(b) Jefferson Davis

(c) Stephen Douglas

92

A N S W E R

(b) Rebels filled the Mississippi seat of former Confederate president Jefferson Davis. In all, twenty-two blacks were elected to Congress during the 1800s, and not one of them was from the North. They all represented states that had been part of the Confederacy.

93 When was the submarine first used in U.S. warfare?

(a) The Revolutionary War

(b) The Civil War

(c) World War I

93

A N S W E R

The surprising answer is **(a)** the Revolutionary War. Using a hand-powered, one-man sub, a Connecticut inventor named David Bushnell attached a mine to the British flagship of Admiral Howe while it was anchored in New York Harbor. The attack failed when the mine floated off before it exploded.

94 Who was the first president to travel outside the Continental United States while in office?

(a) Washington

(b) Jefferson

(c) Roosevelt

(d) Lincoln

ANSWER

(c) Teddy Roosevelt, who visited Panama in 1906. It so happened that they were building a canal there. Roosevelt said he was more proud of the Panama Canal than of anything else he accomplished during his administration.

★ ★ ★ ★ ★ ★ ★ ★

95 Only twelve men have ever walked on the moon. Everyone knows that Neil Armstrong was the first. Who was the last man to walk on the moon while on a mission with *Apollo 17* in 1972?

(a) Eugene Cernan

(b) Harrison Schmitt

(c) James Irwin

95

ANSWER

Jim Irwin wasn't on *Apollo 17*. And although Harrison Schmitt did stroll around the lunar surface during the mission, Eugene Cernan was the last one to get onto the lunar module. So the correct answer is **(a)**.

96 Who was the first American man to orbit the earth?

(a) Neil Armstrong

(b) Buzz Aldrin

(c) John Glenn

96

ANSWER

(c) John Glenn.

97 Who was *Time* magazine's first man of the year?

(a) Henry Ford

(b) Charles Lindbergh

(c) Calvin Coolidge

(d) Adolf Hitler

97

(b) Charles Lindbergh graced the cover of *Time* magazine in 1927.

98 New Yorkers are always in a rush. In order to get people off the island of Manhattan more quickly, the world's first underwater automobile tunnel opened in New York in 1927. What was the name of this modern marvel?

(a) The Lincoln Tunnel

(b) The Holland Tunnel

(c) The Midtown Tunnel

(d) The Brooklyn Battery Tunnel

98

(b) The Holland Tunnel first opened in 1927 with a toll of 50 cents, enabling vehicles to go from New York to New Jersey in under eight minutes.

99 What was the first video to ever be played on MTV?

(a) "Video Killed the Radio Star" by the Buggles

(b) "Like a Virgin" by Madonna

(c) "Beat It" by Michael Jackson

99

(a) Appropriately enough, the first video to appear on MTV was "Video Killed the Radio Star" by the Buggles.

100 The South has always had a rebellious streak in it, but this state takes the cake as the first state to secede from the Union days after Lincoln's election in 1860. Which state was it?

(a) Virginia

(b) Alabama

(c) South Carolina

(d) Mississippi

100

ANSWER

(c) South Carolina was the first state to break away from the Union.

101 What was the first state to ratify the Constitution?

(a) Delaware

(b) New York

(c) Pennsylvania

(d) New Jersey

101

ANSWER

(a) Delaware.